7 DAY BOOK

KT-461-867

This book is due for return on or before the date last stamped below.
You may renew by telephone. Please quote the Barcode No.
May not be renewed if required by another reader.

Fine: 5p per day

YORK PRESS
322 Old Brompton Road, London SW5 9JH

PEARSON EDUCATION LIMITED
Edinburgh Gate, Harlow,
Essex CM20 2JE, United Kingdom
Associated companies, branches and representatives throughout the world

First published 1998
Second impreesion 2000

ISBN 0–582–32926–6

Dasigned by Vicki Pacey, Trajan Horse, London
Phototypeset by Gem Graphics, Tranance, Mawgan Porth, Cornwall
Colour reproduction and film output by Spectrum Colour
Produced by Addison Weslay Longman China Limited, Hong Kong

CONTENTS

PART ONE

INTRODUCTION

HOW TO STUDY A NOVEL

Studying a novel on your own requires self-discipline and a carefully thought-out work plan in order to be effective.

- You will need to read the novel more than once. Start reading it quickly for pleasure, then read it slowly and thoroughly.

- On your second reading make detailed notes on the plot, characters and themes of the novel. Further readings will generate new ideas and help you to memorise the details of the story.

- Some of the characters will develop as the plot unfolds. How do your responses towards them change during the course of the novel?

- Think about how the novel is narrated. From whose point of view are event described?

- A novel may or may not present events chronologically: the time scheme may be a key to its structure and organisation.

- What part do the settings play in the novel?

- Are words, images or incidents repeated so as to give the work a pattern? Do such patterns help you to understand the novel's themes?

- Identify what styles of language are used in the novel.

- What is the effect of the novel's ending? Is the action completed and closed, or left incomplete and open?

- Does the novel present a moral and just world?

- Cite exact sources for all quotations, whether from the text itself or from critical commentaries. Wherever possible find your own examples from the novel to back up your opinions.

- Always express your ideas in your own words.

This York Note offers an introduction to *Wuthering Heights* and cannot substitute for close reading of the text and the study of secondary sources.

From its earliest reception, Emily Brontë's only novel, *Wuthering Heights*, has provoked intense debate amongst its critics and readers. Flouting the conventions of its day, it was initially reviewed, in January 1848, a month after its publication, in *Douglas Jerrold's Weekly Newspaper* as 'a strange sort of book – baffling all regular criticism'. Since then, arguments have ranged from whether Brontë's vision was social and historical or spiritual and **transcendent**, to whether in fact it is possible, let alone desirable, to formulate a clear set of answers to the questions the novel presents. *Wuthering Heights* is a novel which is full of contradictions, a novel which defies stable readings, which is full of unresolved puzzles, unexplained dreams and unquiet ghosts.

Although profoundly shocking to some of its early readers, the novel nevertheless won some praise, as critics recognised its originality and sureness of touch. However, critical response has been unusually divided as to quite what constitutes the novel's success. Some critics have held that this is a timeless romance, a sweeping vision of high passion and the power of **romantic** love; others have maintained that the novel is deeply imbued with historical concerns, that it inevitably responds to its contemporary social, economic and political context. Frequently, its early critics complained about the novel's moral ambiguity, while reluctant to deny its imaginative power.

Often acknowledged for being a subversive novel, *Wuthering Heights* is a novel in which ghosts and fantasies, dreams and visions subvert the natural or realist narrative. It is a novel in which heroes are unheroic and women are sometimes stronger than men; it is a novel which questions the foundations of marriage and the basis of marriage as women's complete subordination to men; it is a novel in which servants seem freer than their masters, for only Nelly Dean can pass unproblematically from the Heights to the Grange; it is a novel in which the boundaries between heaven and hell, between joy and salvation are reassessed and redrawn; and it is a novel in which traditional gender roles are confused, problematised and exploded, for, as Charlotte Brontë informs us:

> for an example of constancy and tenderness, remark that of Edgar Linton. (Some
> people will think these qualities do not shine so well incarnate in a man as they
> would do in a woman, but Ellis Bell could never be brought to comprehend this
> notion: nothing moved her more than any insinuation that the faithfulness and

clemency, the long-suffering and loving-kindness which are esteemed virtues in the daughters of Eve, become foibles in the sons of Adam.)

(Charlotte Brontë, editor's preface to *Wuthering Heights*, p. xxxv)

Criticisms of the novel that have focused on its 'confusion' and its 'incoherence' have tended to be moral judgements rather than formal. This is a novel of profound moral ambivalence. The villains are not punished any more than the righteous, and indeed it is not often easy to distinguish between the two. There are no simple or straightforward answers to the questions raised by Brontë in *Wuthering Heights*: questions as to whether love or economic necessity must triumph; questions as to whether Heathcliff is the archetypal **romantic** hero, or an intrinsically evil character; questions about the ending of the novel, and how it causes us to reflect upon our initial assumptions.

The discrepancies between the various answers that have been suggested to these questions and the judgements made about the novel may well be perplexing and frustrating, but they also attest to the critical potency of this text. If there were only one way of reading novels, one set of right answers to be elicited, then there would be no point in reading literature. It is the very incompatibility of **discourses** within literary texts that makes literature interesting and worthy of critical attention.

On one level the novel can be read as the supreme celebration of a love story, describing a love which defies authority, social convention, even death. Catherine and Heathcliff's love is famously deferred, never consummated and never translated into the pettiness of daily interactions. Theirs is a love which is idealised and magnified, and, in positing such a relationship, the novel both recognises and explicitly appeals to the desire for perfect love.

However, as Pauline Nester points out in her introduction to the 1995 Penguin Edition:

> while the novel may seem to hold out the promise of such satisfaction on this level, in a more complex and more interesting way it actually investigates rather than exemplifies the romantic cliche of perfect love. (p. x)

The potency of the relationship between Catherine and Heathcliff brings to the novel its focus for examining the boundaries of identity. When Catherine declares to Nelly that she *is* Heathcliff, she offers a radical challenge to conventional notions of selfhood and individuality. This throws into large relief the profound philosophical question of what happens to identity when individuality collides with love, in whatever form: sexual, romantic or religious.

Similarly, at a formal level, the repetitious doubling of names makes individual identity difficult to locate. Individual means indivisible, and Brontë's insistence upon merged or convergent identities destabilises fundamental notions about selfhood and responsibility. Evidently, there are moral as well as social implications in such postulations.

If *Wuthering Heights* suggests that to posit discrete identity is not as straightforward as we would normally imagine, it also takes an unconventional attitude towards gender identity. Clearly, in the sexual potency of his **Byronic** savagery, it is possible to read Heathcliff as the personification of stereotypical masculinity and Isabella, in her tragic **romantic** infatuation with him, as manifesting a version of femininity which provides its exact counterpart. However, in spite of such extremes, gender is demonstrably more equivocal than this: Catherine may adopt a certain version of ladylike femininity, but it is a version that ultimately kills her; Edgar is described as both fair and slight, but he is also referred to as 'the master', and he has the full weight of patriarchal privilege behind him; Heathcliff, by comparison, is an outcast, with no social position until he contrives his own. Linton Heathcliff is depicted as relentlessly effeminate, more convincing as Edgar Linton's daughter than as Heathcliff's son, according to Joseph (p. 205). Equally, Cathy's energy, daring and mobility are more suggestive of conventional masculinity in the nineteenth century.

The novel both appeals to and subverts stereotypical constructions of sex roles by suggesting that strategies for survival are gender-related. So, for example, Heathcliff responds to oppression by plotting revenge, whereas Catherine turns to self-destruction. However, Brontë does not permit us simply to regard one response as inherently masculine and the other as feminine, because she makes clear that these strategies are determined as much by circumstance or opportunity as by gender – Isabella is inclined to violence, but lacks the means to inflict it.

This is a novel then that transgresses boundaries which Western culture has held particularly dear: social and sexual relations; the limits of life and death; personal responsibility; order and chaos; economic value and moral judgement; it is able to do so in part because of the importance of dreams in the novel.

Dreams in this novel are both visionary and inexplicable. They are treated with respect and fear, and this is entirely appropriate for dreams offer the opportunity of presenting a world which operates in quite unpredictable and disturbing ways. Dreams also present us with ways of understanding the world which might otherwise be unthinkable. The novel's violations and reinventions of identity, sexuality and taboo are as uncensored as in a dream: they are free from the restrictions of convention. Dreams do not insist upon one story, they accommodate multiplicity. In dreams contradiction may well be disturbing, but it is not deleted.

Wuthering Heights has also been noted for its generic ambiguity. And it is perhaps precisely this generic uncertainty which continues to beguile and intrigue so many readers. As the comforting pleasure of the familiar, provided by the text's realism, is challenged by the subversive power of the genres of fantasy and horror so the sheer enjoyment of the novel's **romantic** escapism is subtly counterpointed by the confidently combative stand it takes against convention. *Wuthering Heights* is a novel which causes us to reassess our conventional wisdom, to consider the prejudices that we take for granted, to take delight in contradiction, for it is in contradiction that argument, theory and intellectual stimulation find their gratification.

The edition used in these Notes is the Penguin Classics Edition, 1995, edited with an introduction and notes by Pauline Nestor.

Part two

Summaries

Wuthering Heights is Emily Brontë's only novel and it was published together with her sister Anne's novel, *Agnes Grey*, in December 1847 under the androgynous **pseudonyms** Ellis and Acton Bell. The Brontës' decision to use pseudonyms was one they had taken a year earlier with the publication of their poetry, *Poems by Currer, Ellis and Acton Bell*, because they wanted their poetry to receive due critical attention. As Charlotte explained: 'We had a vague impression that authoresses are liable to be looked on with prejudice' (Biographical Notice in *Wuthering Heights*, p. xxvii). The identity of the authors was revealed by Charlotte Brontë as she revised the text of the novel and added her preface to the second edition, published in 1850, two years after Emily Brontë's death. Most contemporary editions of the novel include Charlotte Brontë's prefaces.

Editions of the novel vary as to whether they retain the original two-volume structure, or whether they run the chapters on from one to thirty-four. These notes have assumed the structure of the original version.

Synopsis

The story of *Wuthering Heights* is framed by two narrators, Lockwood, who commences and concludes the narrative, and Nelly Dean, who provides most of the narration.

The deferred passionate relationship between Catherine Earnshaw and Heathcliff is the single dominating feature of *Wuthering Heights*, driving the action of the novel forward in all its inexorable yet surprising directions. This is a dynastic novel, which plots the intertwined fortunes of three generations of the Earnshaws and the Lintons, fortunes which seem to repeat and revise the prime relationship between Catherine and Heathcliff.

The first three chapters detail Lockwood's relationship with his landlord, Heathcliff, and his experience of a sequence of visionary and inexplicable dreams in Heathcliff's home, Wuthering Heights. The narrative then passes to Nelly Dean, who takes us back in time to Heathcliff's arrival at the Heights as a child.

Catherine and Heathcliff grow up as siblings, after Heathcliff is introduced into the Earnshaw household by Catherine's father as a foundling and given the name of a dead son. Their relationship is one of intense identification. When their father dies, Catherine's brother Hindley returns to Wuthering Heights with a wife, Frances, and becomes the master of the house. Hindley's wish to sever the intimacy between Catherine and Heathcliff is given unexpected opportunity when Catherine spends five weeks at the neighbouring house, Thrushcross Grange, following a foot injury from their guard dog. Catherine returns to the Heights transformed into a lady, having made friends with the children of the Grange – Edgar and Isabella. While Catherine has been away, Hindley has systematically degraded Heathcliff, refusing him education, and insisting that he work as a labourer on the grounds. Hindley and Frances have a son, Hareton, and Frances dies shortly afterwards.

The events of the novel all resonate from the choice which Catherine makes to marry Edgar Linton rather than Heathcliff. How this choice is interpreted very much depends upon the critical stand one takes: it is possible to read it as economically inevitable, as profoundly immoral, as socially desirable, or as an act of perverse self-denial. These are not, of course, the only options available.

Following this choice, Heathcliff disappears for three years, and Catherine marries Edgar and moves to Thrushcross Grange. Her marriage to Edgar is described as affectionate, if subdued. Nelly Dean, the housekeeper moves with her from the Heights. When Heathcliff returns he is quite transformed into an imposing and compelling figure of a man. He enraptures Catherine, and captivates Isabella, much to the annoyance of Edgar.

Heathcliff stays at Wuthering Heights, with his former enemy Hindley, with whom he gambles. In spite of Catherine's and Nelly Dean's warnings, Isabella falls in love with Heathcliff and Heathcliff perceives that she might well be his route to seeking revenge upon Edgar for depriving him of Catherine.

Edgar and Heathcliff argue violently, precipitating illness in

Catherine. During the time that Catherine is ill, Heathcliff courts Isabella. Isabella and Heathcliff marry and Edgar disowns his sister.

For two months Edgar nurses Catherine, and there is no word from Isabella or Heathcliff. Then a letter from Isabella to Nelly Dean reveals that they are back at Wuthering Heights, and that the marriage is desperately unhappy. She begs Nelly to visit her.

The second volume commences with a visit from Heathcliff to Catherine. He perceives that her death is both imminent and inevitable. She dies that evening, giving birth to a daughter, Cathy, two months premature.

Isabella runs away from Heathcliff and her oppressive marriage. She departs for the South of England, where a few months later she gives birth to a son, Linton Heathcliff. At about this time Hindley dies leaving Heathcliff alone at the Heights with Hareton, whom Heathcliff treats as cavalierly as Hindley had treated him. When Isabella dies, Linton, now twelve and a sickly effeminate child, returns to Thrushcross Grange with Edgar. Heathcliff sends for him immediately and he is returned to Wuthering Heights to live with his father.

Cathy lives secluded but cherished at Thrushcross Grange, and her cousin's proximity is kept from her. On her sixteenth birthday, however, she chances to meet Heathcliff and Hareton on the moors and returns with them to Wuthering Heights where she is astonished to see Linton.

Heathcliff intends that Cathy and Linton should marry, for that way alone can he gain control of both houses, Wuthering Heights and Thrushcross Grange. Linton is sick and peevish, but Cathy's generous nature ensures that she feels a responsibility to making his life happier, a generosity which Heathcliff exploits fully.

Cathy is forbidden by Edgar to go back to the house, but contrives to write to Linton instead. Eventually though she gets the opportunity to pay him visits undetected by either Edgar or Nelly Dean.

Heathcliff's plan that the two cousins should marry is under time pressure, because Linton is so sick. Heathcliff's determination to revenge drives him to tyranny and eventually he forces a marriage between the two, since he is unable to manipulate events in any other way.

Edgar dies, Thrushcross Grange passes to Linton as the male progeny of Isabella, rather than to Cathy, as the female progeny of Edgar. But when Linton dies shortly afterwards, Heathcliff inherits what would otherwise

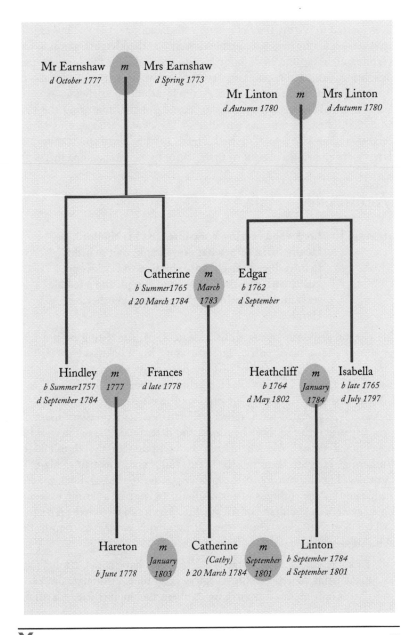

Mr Earnshaw
d October 1777

m

Mrs Earnshaw
d Spring 1773

Mr Linton
d Autumn 1780

m

Mrs Linton
d Autumn 1780

Catherine
b Summer1765
d 20 March 1784

m March 1783

Edgar
b 1762
d September

Hindley
b Summer1757
d September 1784

m 1777

Frances
d late 1778

Heathcliff
b 1764
d May 1802

m January 1784

Isabella
b late 1765
d July 1797

Hareton
b June 1778

m January 1803

Catherine
(Cathy)
b 20 March 1784

m September 1801

Linton
b September 1784
d September 1801

have reverted to Cathy, since she is now his daughter-in-law. Thus cruelly dispossessed, Cathy lives a miserable existence at the Heights spurning any overtures of friendship from both Hareton and Zillah, the housekeeper. This brings us to the point at which Lockwood arrives as tenant of Thrushcross Grange, and introduces himself into the household.

The final three chapters of the second volume, mirroring the first three of the first, restore the narrative to Lockwood, who returns to the Heights a year later, to find that Heathcliff has died and Cathy and Hareton are enjoying a blissful courtship prior to their impending marriage.

VOLUME ONE

CHAPTER 1   **Lockwood visiting Yorkshire pays his landlord, Heathcliff, a somewhat unwelcome visit in order to introduce himself. Introduction to Lockwood, Heathcliff, Heathcliff's servant Joseph and a female servant. Description of the property Wuthering Heights**

The chapter famously opens with the date 1801, suggesting both a new beginning and a diary entry. The narrator, Mr Lockwood, is visiting Yorkshire and is the new tenant of Thrushcross Grange. His landlord, who lives at Wuthering Heights, is Heathcliff, described by Lockwood as 'a dark-skinned gipsy in aspect, in dress and manners a gentleman' (p. 5). Lockwood is revealed as a rather self-satisfied and precious narrator, peculiarly insensitive to those he meets, and determined to see the world in conventional terms. We are offered a description of the threshold of Wuthering Heights, bearing the date 1500 and the name Hareton Earnshaw, but the history of the property is postponed as Lockwood is intimidated by the surliness of his landlord. In spite of a hostile welcome and an evident lack of desire on Heathcliff's part for the visit to be repeated, Lockwood nevertheless closes the chapter with a vow to return the following day.

As some critics, most notably C.P. Sanger, have noted, Brontë is at great pains to reflect chronological exactitude. Although the exact date is only mentioned three times, there are innumerable indications such as seasonal references and ages of characters which alert us to the complex time shifts in this novel. Employing the use of the double narratives of Lockwood and Nelly (Nelly's narrative commences part way through the fourth chapter) was also a highly original technique, permitting Brontë to comment upon the nature of narratorial perspective.

penetralium the innermost parts or recesses of the building, most especially a temple. This use of a highly specialised Latinate term is indicative of Lockwood's education and sophistication

'I never told my love' a reference to *Twelfth Night*, Act II, Scene 4, lines 114–16, which establishes Lockwood as an educated narrator

gnarl snarl

CHAPTER 2   **Lockwood repeats his visit to the Heights and meets Hareton and Catherine Heathcliff. Lockwood is obliged to spend the night as a guest at the Heights owing to hostile weather conditions**

Lockwood again visits Wuthering Heights the following afternoon, and arrives just as a snow shower begins. At first his way into the house is barred, and Joseph, hearing Lockwood's commotion, is most unhelpful. Lockwood meets, but is not introduced to, Hareton, who takes him in round the back. He also meets Cathy Heathcliff, 'the missis', who is spectacularly surly. Hareton invites Lockwood to sit down. In stilted conversation with Cathy, Lockwood mistakes a heap of dead rabbits for a cushion full of cats, revealing him as an unreliable observer. Lockwood antagonises Hareton by trying to guess at the family and social relationships, and in the end Heathcliff reluctantly explains that both his wife and his son are dead, and that Cathy is his daughter-in-law.

Meanwhile the snow shower has turned into a blizzard, and Lockwood is finally obliged to stay the night. It is clear that he is most unwelcome, but Zillah, the housekeeper, takes pity on him and shows him to a bedroom.

This chapter clearly conveys the structural and social differences between Lockwood's expectations and the conventions he comes into contact with in Yorkshire. His desire to dine at five, for example, reflects a non-labouring lifestyle. Through the character of Joseph, Brontë provides a convincing rendition of Yorkshire dialect, which again serves to position Lockwood as an outsider, unable to comprehend the ordinary **discourse** of the region. Equipped with only his conventional notions of the world, Lockwood's pitiful misreading of the domestic situation stands as a warning against the adequacy of conventionality as a reliable reading of the world.

Note another reference to Shakespeare on p. 17 – *King Lear*, Act II, Scene 4, lines 279–82.

Whet are ye for? What do you want?

i' t' fowld in the field

ut' laithe in the barn

flaysome fearful

discussed ate

un war and worse

a nowt a nothing, useless

agait afoot

nobbut strictly: nothing but; here: no-one but

shoo she

Wisht! Hush!

CHAPTER 3   **Lockwood sleeps in a forbidden, secret room, and encounters the ghost of Catherine, much to Heathcliff's distress**

Zillah shows Lockwood to a room at the top of the house which, she confides, is both secret and forbidden. The room is home to a sparse mildewed library, which Lockwood peruses just before sleep. He also remarks upon the window-ledge which is covered with the name Catherine, in a number of manifestations: Catherine Earnshaw, Catherine Linton, Catherine Heathcliff. As he falls asleep, these versions of the name seem to Lockwood to swarm 'as vivid as spectres' (p. 20). He rouses himself to read through some of the books, and is surprised to discover the library is itself a **palimpsest**, every margin and space consumed with another writing, a text of Catherine's diary. Lockwood reads both the printed text: *Seventy Times Seven, and the First of the Seventy-first: a Pious Discourse* *delivered by the Rev. Jabes Branderham in the Chapel of Gimmerden Sough*, and the handwritten diary until he falls asleep.

While asleep he has two dreams:
First Dream: Lockwood is travelling with Joseph as his guide, when he discovers they are going not home but to see the Rev. Jabes Branderham preach. One of them, either Lockwood, or Joseph or the preacher, has committed the first of the seventy-first sins and is to be publicly denounced or excommunicated. Lockwood remonstrates with the preacher and reveals himself to be the sinner. He wakens from the dream to conclude that his sleep had been disturbed by the rapping of a branch against the window.

Second Dream: in this dream Lockwood is still aware of the branch tapping the window and resolves to stop it; however, when he reaches for the branch, his hand closes upon the icy fingers of a child. The child refuses to let go and begs to be allowed into the room. She identifies herself as Catherine Linton. In his terror Lockwood scrapes the hand backwards and forwards across the broken windowpane until the blood flows, the child releases her grip and Lockwood withdraws but cannot shut out her lament that she has been waiting for twenty years to get back in the room. Finally he cries out in fear and his cry brings Heathcliff to the scene. Heathcliff rushes into the room and is dismayed to find Lockwood installed.

Neither Lockwood nor Heathcliff can sleep for the rest of the night, and Lockwood leaves Heathcliff in the room grieving for his 'heart's darling' (p. 29), while he goes down to the kitchen, presently to be joined by Joseph and Hareton.

Lockwood declines breakfast and makes his move back to Thrushcross Grange at dawn. Heathcliff accompanies him back across the moors and leaves him at the gate to the Grange, whereupon Lockwood manages to double the distance to the house, losing himself among the trees. He returns to Thrushcross Grange full of self-pity feeling himself to be 'as feeble as a kitten' (p. 32), to be attended by his housekeeper, Nelly Dean.

This is a chapter which has received much critical attention. Containing Lockwood's two dreams, it clearly lends itself to a **psychoanalytical** reading, a reading which treats the novel itself like a dream, a fiction of the mind, which must be interpreted before its meaning can be clearly apprehended. As Philip K. Wion points out in his psychoanalytic reading of the novel, dreams and hallucinations are forms of seeing in which the boundaries between the self and the world are broken down, since in dreams, the dreamer is often both an observer and a participant. The names inscribed upon the windowsill might similarly be read as an indicator of the conflicting elements of Catherine's identity.

J. Hillis Miller's influential **deconstructive** reading of the chapter discusses the **palimpsestic** nature of the texts, in which each text can be seen as a commentary upon a previous one, in a movement which extends inexorably back with no primary text ever reached. His reading follows this trajectory: Catherine's diary is described by Lockwood as a commentary, written in the margins of Branderham's sermon. That sermon is itself a commentary upon text of the New Testament in which Jesus enjoins his followers to forgive seventy times seven. The first of the seventy-first is therefore to be understood as the unpardonable sin. Jesus's injunction is his interpretation of the nature of forgiveness, and includes a reading of several phrases from the Old Testament. Jesus's interpretation is characteristically accompanied by a **parable**. A parable is an interpretation by means of a story which illustrates that which is to be interpreted.

Wuthering Heights can similarly be read as a **parable**, then, in that it too is Lockwood's narration of a story which is adjacent to or in the margins of the enigmatic events which he is trying to understand. Miller's reading focuses attention on the role of margins in this novel; he comments upon the difficulty of identifying the exact beginning of the novel, prefaced as it is by so many introductions. Lockwood's dreams can be seen as being exemplary of precisely this difficulty of locating an exact beginning or precise meaning.

The description of Lockwood as a kitten serves to identify him as similar to Edgar who is described as a cat in Chapter 8.

nut o'ered not over
lugs ears
laiking playing

scroop the spine of a book
pawsed his fit kicked his feet
laced thrashed
Grimalkin name of a cat, as for example the witches' cat Greymalkin, in *Macbeth*

CHAPTER 4

Lockwood engages his housekeeper Nelly Dean to tell him the story of the inhabitants of Wuthering Heights, whereupon he and we learn something of Heathcliff's history and the family relationships that currently prevail

The chapter commences with Lockwood finally admitting his need for human company and prevailing upon Nelly Dean to entertain him with local gossip. At this point Nelly Dean takes over the role of narrator. Primarily Lockwood is interested in the story of Wuthering Heights, and so we learn something of the early history of Catherine and Heathcliff and the various family relationships, both contemporary and historical. We learn that Cathy Heathcliff, condescendingly described by Lockwood as 'that pretty girl-widow' (p. 33) had married Heathcliff's son, and that her maiden name had been Linton. We learn that she is the last of the Lintons as Hareton is the last of the Earnshaws. Nelly hints that Heathcliff has cheated Hareton out of his rightful inheritance.

Nelly's story begins with the arrival of Heathcliff to the Heights as a child. Old Mr Earnshaw, Catherine's father returns to his family from a trip to Liverpool with the child as a 'gift from God' (p. 36). Other preliminary observations about Heathcliff remark him as a 'gipsy brat' (p. 37) and 'a dirty ragged black-haired child' (p. 36).

Earnshaw's children, Catherine and Hindley immediately dislike the newcomer because the presents which their father had promised them, a fiddle for Hindley and a whip for Catherine, had been either crushed or lost on the way home. Mrs Earnshaw too is appalled at the idea of having another child to feed and clothe. But Mr Earnshaw is adamant and the 'cuckoo' (p. 35) remains as a family member and is christened Heathcliff after a son who had died in childhood. The name Heathcliff serves the child as both Christian and surname from that point on.

Eventually he and Catherine become firm friends, but his presence in the household seems divisive, as Hindley continues to hate him and Mr

Earnshaw makes him his favourite. Two years later Mrs Earnshaw dies and the children all fall sick with the measles. This endears Heathcliff to Nelly Dean as he is most uncomplaining, unlike Hindley and Catherine. The chapter closes with the incident of the two colts. Heathcliff takes the best and, when his falls lame, takes Hindley's. Hindley's behaviour towards Heathcliff is brutish and violent. Heathcliff, once he gets his way is self-contained and apparently unvindictive, though tantalisingly Nelly confides that in this assessment she was 'deceived, completely' (p. 40).

The most significant aspect of this chapter is the change of narrator from Lockwood, whom we have come to perceive as unreliable, to Nelly Dean who has the advantage of having lived with the main protagonists and who is thus able to gloss their characters for Lockwood. This doubling of narrator acts, as J. Hillis Miller reminds us, as a caution to the overconfident reader, for it immediately unsettles our certainty that the narrator's voice is neutral or trustworthy. This device of an external masculine narrative framing and legitimating an internal feminine narrative was also used by Anne Brontë in *The Tenant of Wildfell Hall*, and can be seen in relation to Brontë's use of the masculine **pseudonym** to legitimate her novel.

The arrival of Heathcliff at the Heights has been the focus of much critical attention. In *The Madwoman in the Attic: The Woman Writer and the Nineteenth-Century Literary Imagination*, Sandra Gilbert and Susan Gubar read this arrival in terms of its gender implications, paying attention to the whip as a symbol of masculinity, which Catherine has requested and which is lost only to be replaced by Heathcliff. In *Myths of Power: A Marxist Study of the Brontës*, a **marxist** reading of the novel, Terry Eagleton sees Heathcliff's presence at the Heights as both radical and random. Because Heathcliff's origins are so obscure, and because his family relationships place him outside the conventional social structure of the family, he is available to be loved or hated for himself. His lack of social status or clear social role, coupled with Mr Earnshaw's favouritism, destabilises any certainty about inheritance and genealogy, causing Hindley to feel, rightly, threatened, and Catherine, equally rightly, strengthened.

strike my colours a naval term meaning to show the flag for surrender

dunnock sparrow

flighted frightened

CHAPTER 5   **Nelly Dean recounts how the family relationships develop as Mr Earnshaw's health fails. First sustained description of Catherine**

As Mr Earnshaw's health begins to fail his partiality towards Heathcliff becomes even more pronounced. Hindley continues to scorn Heathcliff, which enrages his enfeebled father. The family curate, who has supplemented his income by teaching the Earnshaw children advises that Hindley be set to college, to which Earnshaw agrees, though considers his eldest son unlikely to succeed at anything.

The first description of Catherine shows her as beautiful, lively and wayward, but with a good heart: 'A wild, wick slip she was – but she had the bonniest eye, and the sweetest smile, and the lightest foot in the parish; and after all, I believe she meant no harm' (p. 42). Mr Earnshaw dies quietly one October evening. Both Catherine and Heathcliff are utterly distraught, and comfort one another.

The focus of this chapter is Catherine's relationships with her father and Heathcliff of whom, Nelly avers, Catherine is much too fond. However, the description of Catherine as deliberately infuriating and rebellious, and indeed of Heathcliff as some sort of devilish progeny is counterbalanced by their response to her father's death, which Nelly describes as both anguished and innocent. Contradiction is seen to be an integral part of the way in which people relate to each other.

made the living answer supplemented his income

wick lively

frame hurry

CHAPTER 6   **Hindley returns as the master of the Heights, with a wife. He endeavours to make Heathcliff's life a misery, but Catherine and Heathcliff remain inseparable and wild. Catherine is hurt on one of their escapades and remains at the neighbouring house, Thrushcross Grange, until she is considered well enough to return to the Heights**

Hindley comes home for the funeral accompanied by a wife, Frances, who is described as poor, ill and silly. As the new master of the Heights, Hindley finds vent for all his old hatred of Heathcliff. He denies him an education, insists that he should labour out of doors and makes him live with the servants. None of this at all detracts from Catherine and Heathcliff's bond, and they are united in their 'naughtiness'. One night when they cannot be found Hindley instructs that the doors be bolted against them. When Heathcliff returns alone, it emerges that Catherine has remained at Thrushcross Grange where they have been peeping in at the Lintons, who live there. There follows the first introduction to Edgar Linton and his sister Isabella, as 'petted things' (p. 48). Once observed, they are set upon by the guard dogs and Catherine is caught by the ankle and savaged, thus she is unable to return to the Heights with Heathcliff. The next day Mr Linton remonstrates with Hindley for being unable to run his household properly, Heathcliff is forbidden to talk to Catherine, and Frances undertakes to keep Catherine in due restraint.

The chronology of this chapter takes us back to the point in time of Catherine's diaries, read by Lockwood in Chapter 3.

Critical attention to this chapter has often focused upon the structural differences between Thrushcross Grange and Wuthering Heights. The splendid, cultivated and civilised atmosphere at the Grange is compared with the rough indiscipline of the Heights. Most famously David Cecil has argued that the differences between the Heights and the Grange can be thought of as corresponding to a **metaphysical** opposition between storm and calm. And yet, as Gilbert and Gubar point out the violence which one might naturally associate with the Heights is no less present at the Grange. They argue that Catherine, for example, does not so much willingly enter the world of Thrushcross Grange, as be seized by it. Indeed, as Terry Eagleton points out, the more property one has, the more ferociously one needs to protect it.

foreigners strangers
lascar east-Indian seaman
negus hot toddy made of wine and water

CHAPTER 7 **Catherine returns from her five week stay at Thrushcross Grange, transformed into a lady. Heathcliff has been systematically further debased by Hindley during this time. End of chapter reminds us that this is a story being related to Lockwood by Nelly Dean**

Catherine stays at Thrushcross Grange for five weeks until she is deemed healthy, both in body and manners. She returns to the Heights a very 'dignified person' (p. 52) dressed in fine clothes and quite transformed from the person she had been. Heathcliff, by contrast, is forbiddingly unkempt, but Catherine's love of him is undiminished and she embraces him immediately. The Linton children have been invited over the next day in order to thank them for tending Catherine. Heathcliff begs Nelly to make him decent. Hindley and Edgar Linton combine to discredit and humiliate Heathcliff, who retaliates violently. Heathcliff is dismissed and Catherine apparently unfeelingly continues to have tea with her new friends. Eventually she creeps away from the tea party to be with Heathcliff, and Heathcliff plots his revenge on Hindley.

Finally Nelly Dean interrupts her narrative to focus upon Lockwood, who requires her to continue her story even though the hour is late. Lockwood comments on the class and type of people he has encountered in the region, and Nelly recalls to us his hasty judgements and his condescension by remarking that he 'could not open a book in this library that [she had] not looked into' (p. 62).

Lockwood's failure to read Nelly Dean in any terms other than the conventions of class is further reinforced by his insensitivity to Nelly's hours of sleep and work. She characteristically deflates his pompous exposition upon the type of people native to the region by drawing attention to both her level of formal education and the lessons learned from the exacting discipline of her life.

cant lively

CHAPTER 8   Hindley's son Hareton is born. Frances Earnshaw dies of consumption and Hindley declines even further into recklessness. The relationship between Catherine and Edgar is developed and the tension between Edgar and Heathcliff is intensified

In June 1778 Hareton Earnshaw is born as the son to Hindley and Frances. Not long afterwards Frances dies of consumption and Nelly Dean is bidden to Wuthering Heights to act as nursemaid to the baby. Hindley goes into a decline at the death of his wife and relinquishes himself to drinking and dissolute behaviour. Catherine is now fifteen years old and Edgar Linton has taken to calling on her. Nelly's account of Edgar is that he 'wanted spirit in general' (p. 66). Nelly details Catherine's conflicting alliances with both Heathcliff and Edgar. Catherine's reluctance for them to meet stems from the feeling that their differences only highlight her own internal conflicts. Catherine and Heathcliff quarrel as she chooses to spend more time with the Lintons than with him, and when Edgar comes to call Catherine reacts badly to Nelly's presence in the room, pinching her and slapping her face, which she then promptly lies about. Edgar is shocked at her behaviour and attempts to intervene, earning himself a box on the ears. Edgar makes to leave, but in spite of himself cannot bear to part with her and eventually only leaves when Hindley returns home drunk.

This chapter first explicitly details the central conflict of the novel, the choice that Catherine has to make between Heathcliff and Edgar Linton. The choice is pivotal to all the events in the novel, and has been variously seen as a choice between passion and social status, authenticity and bad faith, sex and sublimation, risk and security, nature and culture, spirituality and economics. The choice is almost always seen as being between two incompatible ways of life.

Dorothy Van Ghent in her **formalist** analysis of the novel *The English Novel: Form and Function* focuses her attention upon the significance of the numerous windows and doors in this novel, arguing that such formal boundaries represent the tension between these two conflicting realities. She draws attention to the ways in which different characters aim to cross these physical boundaries and unite the two kinds of reality, and argues that although for Catherine Earnshaw the attempt results in her death, suggesting that the choice is really about unreconcilable realities, by the end of the novel, Catherine Heathcliff does succeed in achieving the domestic romance.

rush of a lass slip of a girl

loading lime a procedure to make the ground more fertile

CHAPTER 9   **Catherine makes her choice between Edgar and Heathcliff and chooses Edgar. Heathcliff disappears. Catherine catches a fever and goes once more to recuperate at the Grange. Three years later, when Edgar is master of the Grange, he marries Catherine. Nelly reluctantly leaves Hareton and goes with Catherine to the Grange**

Heathcliff and Hindley's relationship deteriorates even further. Hindley is abusive and violent to everyone, threatens Nelly with a carving knife and shows no affection for his son. Hareton falls from Hindley's arms over the stairwell only to be caught by Heathcliff who cannot believe that he has done Hindley a favour. After this Heathcliff retires to the dark end of the kitchen where he remains unobserved and silent. Catherine comes in and confesses to Nelly that Edgar has asked her to marry him. She has already given Edgar her answer, but nevertheless wishes Nelly to say what the answer should have been. There follows an exposition on the nature of love during which Catherine shows her feelings for Edgar to be based upon his looks, his disposition and his wealth. She believes that she has no more business to marry him than she has a right to heaven. She announces that it would degrade her to marry Heathcliff, whereupon Heathcliff leaves the kitchen and the household. After his departure, which goes unobserved by Catherine, she goes on to say how she will never forsake Heathcliff, and the chapter contains the famous line: 'Nelly, I *am* Heathcliff' (p. 82).

Nelly reveals to Catherine that Heathcliff has overheard part of what she had said and Catherine distressed at the possible consequences rushes out into the night to try and find him. She sits the whole night outside, catches a chill and becomes dangerously ill with a fever. Mrs Linton insists that she return to Thrushcross Grange to convalesce, but she and her husband then both catch the fever and die, leaving Edgar as the master of the Grange. Once again Catherine returns to the Heights haughtier than she left.

Three years later, during which time Heathcliff has never returned, Catherine marries Edgar and Hindley bids Nelly to accompany her against her will to Thrushcross Grange, leaving Hareton to the negligent and cruel inclinations of his father, alone in Wuthering Heights. The final paragraph of the chapter returns the narrative to Lockwood, who observes the housekeeper note the time and they repair to their beds.

The central dichotomy of the novel is revealed here as being a choice about love and the nature of love. Catherine expounds her thoughts on love through a dream she has had about being unfit to enter heaven. **Psychoanalytic** critics have focused their attention on the dreams in this novel and the ways in which desire is sublimated into other, destructive, channels. Other critics such as **marxist** and **feminist** critics have read this decision in terms of its political ramifications.

Catherine's declaration of love for Heathcliff comes at precisely the moment that she has chosen to marry Edgar, and at the point at which Heathcliff disappears from their lives. It is therefore possible to read this as indicative of the ways in which the consummation of passion is endlessly deferred in favour of social convention and restraint.

grat wept
mools earth, soil, particularly the soil of a grave
The fate of Milo Milo was a Greek athlete who attempted to tear an oak in two, but found himself trapped when the cleft closed over his hands
girt great, big
eedle idle
seeght sight
war worse
rigs ridges
plottered blundered
offald worthless
starving frozen
bog-hoile hole in the marsh
gentle and simple the upper and lower class
wer our

CHAPTER 10   **Catherine Earnshaw now married to Edgar Linton, lives in relative luxury and peace with Edgar and his sister Isabella. Heathcliff returns to Catherine's immense jubilation. Heathcliff staying with Hindley at the Heights. Isabella develops an intense fascination for Heathcliff who does not return the sentiment, but sees that he might use her attraction for him as a way to revenge himself upon Edgar**

The chapter opens with Lockwood feeling most sorry for himself after four weeks of illness and a visit from Heathcliff. He calls for Nelly Dean to resume her narrative. Nelly's story recommences with the marriage of Edgar and Catherine. As Catherine Linton, Catherine's life is one of gentle cultivation, largely because she is endlessly indulged by both Edgar and Isabella. Life is simple and happy until the return of Heathcliff.

Heathcliff's return is the source of fervent joy for Catherine. Nelly details the transformation of Heathcliff into a tall, intelligent man in whom passion is observable but subdued. It emerges that Heathcliff is staying with Hindley Earnshaw at Wuthering Heights, which causes Nelly to be suspicious.

Visits between Heathcliff and Catherine become more frequent and Isabella develops an intense fascination for Heathcliff which irritates Edgar and worries Catherine. Catherine divulges Isabella's attraction to Heathcliff and sows the seed of the idea for revenge into Heathcliff's mind. Heathcliff hints that he will use Isabella's devotion to win his revenge over Edgar.

The return of Heathcliff to the text restores to it some of its sinister energy. It also seems to enliven Catherine and Isabella, taking them out of the atmosphere of the house and onto the moors or up to the Heights. Here, however, Heathcliff has learned to dissemble in order to obtain his desires, and we are reminded of his first visit to Thrushcross Grange, when he despised its inhabitants for their pettiness and selfishness.

Catherine's betrayal of Isabella's confidence to Heathcliff is actually a misrepresentation of what Isabella has declared, for she tells him 'Isabella swears that the love Edgar has for me is nothing to that she entertains for you' (p. 104) whereas Isabella in fact says 'I love him more than you ever loved Edgar' (p. 101). And this misrepresentation too is available for **psychoanalytic** critical analysis.

sizer's place scholarship position at University
sough ditch
Crahnr's 'quest coroner's inquest (into an unnatural death)
t'grand 'sizes the Grand Assizes: here, the day of judgement
girn snarl
pikes gates

CHAPTER 11   **Nelly returns on a whim to the Heights and is appalled to see how it has deteriorated. Heathcliff calls at the Grange and makes overtures to Isabella, displeasing both Catherine and Edgar. Fierce arguments between Catherine, Edgar and Heathcliff induce Catherine to retire to her bed**

Reminiscence marks the opening of this chapter as Nelly Dean fondly remembers both her own childhood with Hindley and her affection for Hareton. Ten months have passed since she left the Heights and now she returns there on a whim to observe it and its inhabitants once more. Hareton, though barely more than five, curses her. Heathcliff, it emerges, has set son against father and is breeding insurrection in the already unhappy household. When Heathcliff appears, Nelly returns swiftly back to the Grange.

Heathcliff's next visit to the Grange sees him capitalise upon Isabella's affection. Catherine requests him to desist from his attentions to Isabella if he wishes to remain welcome, and he and Catherine argue. Heathcliff tells Catherine that she has behaved abominably to him, and that he is set on revenge against the Lintons. Edgar, hearing of Catherine's distress, resolves to throw Heathcliff out. They come to blows and Catherine retires to her bed claiming herself to be 'in danger of being seriously ill' (p. 115). Forced to choose between Edgar and Heathcliff, she threatens to break their hearts by breaking her own. Nelly treats Catherine's outburst as histrionics and fails to take her threatened illness seriously. Catherine departs to her room and refuses any nourishment for the next two days. Edgar retires to the library and tries to dissuade Isabella from her infatuation with Heathcliff, claiming that if she continues in it, then he will disown her.

Once again the central choice of the novel takes up the majority of this chapter. Critical attention has focused upon the role of illness as a sign for femininity in the nineteenth century. Emily Brontë can be seen to be writing about illness as a female strategy here: rather than indicating simply weakness, illness becomes a way of for Catherine to influence the actions of both Edgar and Heathcliff.

barn child
sandpillar milestone

CHAPTER 12　　**Catherine is truly ill. Isabella leaves secretly to marry Heathcliff. Edgar disowns Isabella**

Isabella mopes; Edgar reads; Catherine starves herself. After three days Catherine is convinced she is dying, and is incredulous at Edgar's apparent unconcern. Edgar is so far ignorant of Catherine's condition, since Nelly Dean still believes Catherine's illness to be manufactured in order to manipulate. Now, however, Nelly recalls Catherine's earlier illness and begins to be alarmed for her as Catherine starts to hallucinate. Catherine is delirious and feverish and Edgar, upon entering her room, is horrified at her condition. He blames Nelly for her deterioration, and Nelly goes into the garden to find Isabella's favourite dog hanging from a tree, almost dead. Nelly summons the doctor to attend to Catherine, and the doctor informs her that Isabella and Heathcliff have been having secret nightly trysts and intend to elope. Nelly returns to the Grange to find that Isabella has already left with Heathcliff, but does not tell Edgar because he is so worried about Catherine. The next day Edgar learns of Isabella's departure and disowns her.

Critical attention might well be devoted to the role of Nelly Dean in this chapter, since she is the person who controls all the key critical information: Catherine's illness and Isabella's departure.

Nelly's assumption that Catherine's illness is invented by her in order to manipulate gives credence to the reading that women in the nineteenth century could use frailty as a strength. However, it is a strategy which Brontë shows to have devastating consequences.

Edgar's retirement to the library after the confrontation between himself and Heathcliff, and his ignorance of Catherine's illness has been commented upon as part of the conflict between experience and culture in the novel. Edgar counters his interaction with the real by submerging himself in literature. Such a critical position of course assumes that literature is not part of the 'real'.

caps outshines

pigeon feathers referral to a superstition that the soul of a dying person could not leave the body if the mattress or pillow were stuffed with pigeon feathers

elf-bolts flint arrowheads

CHAPTER 13   Catherine diagnosed as having brain-fever. Edgar nurses her devotedly. Letters from Isabella to Edgar and Nelly suggest that she quickly regrets her decision to elope with Heathcliff. It transpires that they are both now living back at the Heights. Isabella is without an ally there, and begs Nelly to call

For two months Isabella and Heathcliff remain absent. Catherine is diagnosed as having brain-fever and is nursed devotedly by Edgar, under whose ministrations she slowly begins to improve. Six weeks after their departure Isabella writes to Edgar a letter which ends with a secret pencilled note begging for reconciliation. He ignores the request. She then writes to Nelly, and Nelly now reads this letter to Lockwood. It commences with the information that Isabella and Heathcliff are back at Wuthering Heights as Hindley is intent on winning back from Heathcliff all the money he has lost to him through gambling. Isabella perceives herself to be both friendless and abused in her relationships with Heathcliff. Hindley shows Isabella a gun with which he intends to kill Heathcliff, and her reaction to this weapon is one of covetousness rather than horror. Heathcliff has heard of Catherine's illness and blames Edgar for it, promising that Isabella shall be her proxy in suffering. The letter and the chapter end with an entreaty from Isabella to Nelly Dean to call on her at Wuthering Heights.

The reference to the gun, which Isabella views with desire rather than horror is again indicative that violence is as much a part of the civilised life (which Isabella has hitherto represented) as it is a part of the rude brutality of the Heights. Isabella's devotion to Heathcliff results in her destruction and despair, and this is contrasted both with Edgar's devotion to Catherine, and also Catherine's choice of social status over passion. Isabella's inability to partake of the food at Wuthering Heights because it is too coarse for her can be read as indicative of her unlikeliness to be nourished or sustained by life with Heathcliff.

mim prim

minching and munching affected ways

flitting moving house

thible stirring stick or spoon

nave fist

pale t'guilp off skim the froth off

deaved aht knocked out

meeterly properly

mells meddles

madling fool

pining starving

plisky tantrum

CHAPTER 14   **Nelly goes to see Isabella as requested. Heathcliff determines to see Catherine and Nelly reluctantly agrees to act as intermediary. Time switches to the present. The doctor calls on Lockwood, and Lockwood reflects that he must be cautious of falling in love with the present Catherine for fear that she should resemble the first**

Nelly informs Edgar of Isabella's predicament, but he refuses to treat her as kin. Nelly pays a visit to Isabella at Wuthering Heights and comments upon the general air of neglect and disrepair. Heathcliff enquires about Catherine and resolves to see her, whether permission is granted or not. Isabella defends Edgar, but is humiliated by Heathcliff, and departs. Nelly is finally prevailed upon by Heathcliff to act as intermediary between himself and Catherine.

At the end of the chapter the narrative is once more restored to Lockwood, and the present, and Lockwood reminds himself that the lesson he must take from Nelly Dean's story is not to fall in love with Catherine Heathcliff, lest she turns out to be another version of her mother.

Lockwood typically draws the wrong conclusion from Nelly Dean's story, for Nelly Dean sees marriage to someone else as the only escape for Catherine Heathcliff, and is eager to find her another husband. Lockwood however, represents exactly the supersensitive, precious world of the educated, or cultured which is here contrasted with the world of passion and experience.

Isabella's position as a dependant upon Heathcliff is made clear in two passages: firstly when Heathcliff asserts the lengths he has gone to in order to prevent Isabella claiming a separation (p. 149). In fact the effort would not have been considerable, since as John Stuart Mill notes in *The Subjection of Women* in 1869, the position of women within marriage was worse than that of slaves. The second passage makes reference to Isabella's mental health (p. 150) and refers to the practice of incarcerating women as mentally ill, notwithstanding any evidence to the contrary.

brach she-dog; bitch
dree cheerless

VOLUME TWO

CHAPTER 1   **Lockwood resumes the narrative only to impersonate that of Nelly Dean. The narrative recommences with Heathcliff's visit to Catherine which upon discovery by Edgar reduces Catherine to fainting and further illness**

Nelly returns to Thrushcross Grange and arranges matters so that the household is empty apart from herself and Catherine, in order that Heathcliff might pay his visit. On seeing Catherine, Heathcliff despairs, perceiving that she is certainly going to die. The conversation and interaction between Catherine and Heathcliff ricochets between love and death, and they fall on each other in passionate embrace, while talking of going to the grave. Nelly, nervous that the rest of the members of the household will return and her part in the deception will be exposed, grows anxious for Heathcliff to leave, but Catherine begs him to stay. Catherine faints in Heathcliff's arms just as Edgar Linton enters. When they finally manage to revive Catherine, Heathcliff has departed, but resolves to stay in the garden until Nelly can bring him news of Catherine.

Nelly is once again a catalyst for action as she traffics between Wuthering Heights and Thrushcross Grange. The narration which throughout has properly belonged to Lockwood, as the opening to this second volume reminds us, is nevertheless more credibly Nelly Dean's. The opening chapter of this second volume highlights the drama of the conflicts and correspondences between sexuality and death. It is possible to draw parallels between the concerns of this chapter and concerns which dominate Brontë's poetry, not least the longing to escape this world, either through love or death.

CHAPTER 2   Catherine's daughter Cathy Linton born the same night, two months prematurely. Catherine dies in childbirth. Heathcliff knows the news even before Nelly tells him. Funeral one week later

That night Catherine goes into labour two months early and gives birth to a daughter, named Catherine after her mother. Catherine, however, dies in childbirth and Edgar is so grieved by Catherine's death that he cannot welcome his daughter. Heathcliff cries that he cannot live without Catherine, she is his life and soul, which echoes her previous declaration of love for him in Chapter 9.

The funeral takes place a week later, and although Hindley Earnshaw is invited, Isabella is not. Catherine is buried on a grassy slope in the corner of the graveyard nearest the moor.

Reading retrospectively it is possible to see Heathcliff's despair upon seeing Catherine again being provoked not only by his perception of her certain death, but also by his perception of her pregnancy. Such a reading would support the position which argues for the structural correspondences between sex and death.

An historical reading of the chapter would also highlight the dangers of childbirth for women in the nineteenth century.

Nelly Dean also comments upon the consequences of Catherine's death for the inheritance laws. Old Mr Linton has bequeathed his property to Isabella and subsequently to her male offspring should Edgar fail to have a son.

C.P. Sanger has commented upon the very detailed knowledge that Brontë displays of the inheritance laws of the nineteenth century. This knowledge is crucial to the plot of *Wuthering Heights* since according to this law Catherine Linton cannot inherit Thrushcross Grange when her father dies. Instead the property automatically passes to the male progeny of Isabella. However, should there be no male progeny, or should that son die, the property would then revert to Catherine Linton. It is for this reason that Heathcliff is so intent upon the marriage between Catherine and Linton, for as his daughter-in-law her property becomes his.

For the sake of clarity the older Catherine will be referred to as Catherine and the younger as Cathy.

ousel blackbird

CHAPTER 3   **Hindley Earnshaw dies shortly after Catherine. Isabella leaves Heathcliff for the South of England where, a few months later, her son, Linton, is born. Heathcliff, now living alone at the Heights with Hareton, learns of his son's birth through the servants' gossip**

The day of the funeral marks the beginning of poor weather. Edgar keeps to his room, and Nelly nurses the sick baby into strength. One evening Isabella bursts in unannounced having run away from Heathcliff. She is *en route* to the South having fled Heathcliff and the Heights. She throws her wedding ring into the fire and describes the living conditions at the Heights as both physically and morally corrupt. Isabella flees to near London where a few months later she gives birth to a son. Heathcliff learns of his son's birth through servants' gossip. Nelly briefly interrupts the chronology of the narrative to interpose that Isabella dies when her son is twelve. She resumes the chronology with her remark that shortly after Catherine's death Hindley dies, leaving the Heights mortgaged in gambling debts to Heathcliff. Heathcliff now lives alone there with the disinherited Hareton.

Heathcliff has now gained control of Wuthering Heights, having arrived as a presumed orphan, and having been humiliated by his lack of proper status. Hareton, who should be the Heights' rightful inheritor, is dependent upon Heathcliff, who uses the opportunity to repeat the abuse that he himself suffered as someone of no social property.

girned snarled

at the cross-roads the place of burial for those who commit suicide

taen tent taken care

CHAPTER 4   **Twelve years pass. Edgar receives a letter from Isabella informing him that she is dying. He brings Linton home to the Grange at Isabella's request. During the time he is away Cathy ventures to Wuthering Heights and meets Hareton**

Nelly describes the next twelve years as being very happy ones, bringing up Cathy who lives a loving and protected life at the Grange, never venturing beyond its boundaries. Edgar receives a letter from Isabella, informing him that she is dying. He complies with her request that he bring her son, Linton, back to the Grange. Edgar is away for three weeks organising Isabella's funeral and Linton's move North. During this time Cathy ventures beyond the confines of the Grange and is eventually tracked down to Wuthering Heights, where she meets Hareton. She is horrified to learn that he too is her cousin. Nelly Dean is very annoyed with Cathy and impresses upon her that she must not inform her father of her newfound knowledge or he might order Nelly to leave his employment.

Both the Grange and the Heights can be read as confining spaces, imprisoning this new generation of Lintons and Earnshaws. Hareton is confined by Heathcliff who has cheated him of his inheritance, and has refused him any education; and Cathy is confined by the protective nature of life at the Grange, beyond whose boundaries she is not permitted to wander. Read in terms of the conflict between opposing forces, these confines can be seen as the limits of different kinds of knowledge. Hareton is forbidden knowledge of a formal, literary sort, and Cathy is prohibited from experiencing any life other than that which her father controls. When the two come into confrontation they can neither comprehend nor admit each other.

galloway small horse or pony
wisht be quiet
offald awful or wicked
near mean, ungenerous

CHAPTER 5   **Isabella dies, Edgar returns with Linton. They no sooner arrive back at the Grange than Heathcliff demands Linton's presence at the Heights. Edgar is forced to promise to deliver the boy the following day**

The death of Isabella means that Edgar can return to the Grange with his nephew Linton Heathcliff. Linton is described as both sickly and peevish, a delicate and effeminate child. Their arrival back at the Grange is rapidly followed by Joseph, demanding that Linton be returned to his father and Wuthering Heights. Edgar Linton promises to deliver his nephew to the Heights the following day.

Linton's description as both sickly and effeminate is further reference to the association of femininity with ill-health.

baht without
nowt nothing
maks noa 'cahnt pays no attention to
norther neither
darr dare

CHAPTER 6   **Nelly takes Linton to Wuthering Heights, where Heathcliff professes his profound disappointment in him**

The next day Nelly is detailed to take Linton to Wuthering Heights, and is bidden not to tell Cathy where he is. Cathy is told only that his father has sent for him suddenly. Linton is reluctant to depart and Nelly tries to soften the blow by preparing him positively for meeting his father and Hareton. Heathcliff is unequivocally disappointed in his son. Heathcliff describes his ambition for Linton as being to take over all the property of both the Lintons and the Earnshaws. In spite of the vindictive avarice of this ambition, Nelly takes comfort from the thought that in order to achieve it Heathcliff must take care of his son, and provide him with the education that befits a gentleman of property. Linton repeats his mother's inability to eat the food at Wuthering Heights (Volume I Chapter 13), as it is insufficiently delicate for him. The contrast between Linton and Hareton is pronounced.

As Philip K. Wion has noted in his **psychoanalytic** reading of the novel, *Wuthering Heights* is full of oral imagery. Almost all of the social encounters involve food, and food is one of the signs which signals belonging and acceptance. A delicate appetite might also be read as a reluctance to experience or engage with the sensual or the physical.

mucky dirty

CHAPTER 7   **Cathy's disappointment at the untimely disappearance of her cousin gives way in time to a resigned acceptance. On her sixteenth birthday she encounters Heathcliff and goes back to Wuthering Heights where she sees Linton again and learns of her various relationships. She confronts her father with her newfound knowledge. She learns of Heathcliff's plans for revenge and agrees not to visit the Heights again, but nevertheless conspires to find a way to correspond with Linton**

The chapter opens with Cathy's disappointment at her cousin's departure. Nelly retains some knowledge of Linton via her relationship with the housekeeper at Wuthering Heights, and although Edgar refuses any contact, he nevertheless encourages Nelly to continue to gain such intelligence. Cathy reaches her sixteenth birthday, and on a trip onto the moors accompanied by Nelly, strays onto Heathcliff's land. She encounters both Heathcliff and Hareton, and much against Nelly's will, Heathcliff prevails upon them to return to Wuthering Heights. Heathcliff reveals his plan to Nelly that the two cousins (Linton and Cathy) should marry. Then, should Linton die, ownership of Thrushcross Grange would devolve to Heathcliff. Cathy sees Linton again and learns of her relationship to both Heathcliff and Hareton. Hareton and Linton are compared and contrasted.

Linton and Cathy mock Hareton's lack of knowledge, when it emerges that he cannot read. When Cathy returns home she confronts her father with her newly discovered knowledge and he reveals to her Heathcliff's long-fostered plans for revenge. At the request of her father, Cathy agrees not to return to the Heights, but nevertheless determines to correspond with Linton in spite of this being forbidden. Nelly discovers her secret and threatens to burn the letters or reveal them to Edgar. Cathy chooses the former and ceases the correspondence.

Critical attention has frequently focused on the role of textuality and education in this novel, and this chapter highlights these issues. This is a novel which abounds with forbidden texts, from Catherine's diaries through to Cathy's love letters. Text comes to represent knowledge, and Hareton is abused for his lack of it, or for his inability to control it. All the characters in this novel, including its two narrators, are readers in one sense or another, needing to make sense of the signs before them. Nelly Dean uses her knowledge gained from reading to control events in the novel. As Linda Peterson observes in her introduction to a critical edition of *Wuthering Heights*, Brontë seems ambivalent about the effects of education. On the one hand, the denial of education is seen as a form of social punishment; on the other, the conventional forms of nineteenth-century education are frequently pitted against power, both sexual and physical. In this chapter, Brontë's knowledge of the inheritance laws and the implication they have for women's social position is made explicit.

nab a jutting hill or rock. Often this term comes to name a particular piece of hill or moorland.

gaumless witless, lacking in understanding

faster more firmly

lath weakling

CHAPTER 8   **Edgar Linton develops a chill. Heathcliff again encounters Cathy and informs her that Linton is dying of a broken heart owing to her abrupt termination of their correspondence. Cathy sets out again to see Linton**

The chapter opens with another distinct reference to time, and the seasonal change. Edgar Linton is enfeebled by a chill and is confined indoors. Cathy is left to amuse herself, and sometimes Nelly undertakes to accompany her in her solitude. One day when she and Nelly are out walking, Cathy climbs over a wall and cannot get back. Behind the wall she again encounters Heathcliff who informs her that Linton is dying of a broken heart because she has curtailed all correspondence with him. Cathy's sensitive nature is deeply troubled by both this news and her fears that her father will die of his chill. The next day, she and Nelly set out to pay another visit to Linton.

The chapter includes a number of structural elements that have claimed the attention of **formalist** critics. These include: boundaries, illness, death and responsibility.

Heathcliff's information that Linton is dying of a broken heart is disingenuous, since Linton is physically failing and Heathcliff is desirous of rekindling the love affair between Linton and Cathy so that his plans for revenge are not thwarted.

starved frozen
sackless dispirited
canty lively
Slough of Despond a reference to John Bunyan's *Pilgrim's Progress*

CHAPTER 9   **Cathy and Nelly again visit Wuthering Heights. A quarrel about the nature of marriage. Linton persuades Cathy to return the following day, and because Nelly too falls ill with a chill, Cathy is able to visit Linton unimpaired by any restrictive supervision**

The following day Cathy and Nelly again visit the Heights to find Linton more peevish and delicate than ever. Cathy and Linton quarrel about the nature of marriage. During the quarrel Cathy tells Linton that his parents hated each other, and he informs her that her mother hated her father and loved his. Linton's triumph is succeeded by a prolonged coughing fit which causes both Nelly and Cathy concern. By wheedling and whining and prevailing upon Cathy's sensitive nature, Linton secures a promise from her that she will come and visit him again, a promise Cathy is able to keep because Nelly falls ill with a chill and can no longer supervise her movements.

Here illness is once more cited as a strategy. It is used effectively by Linton to influence Cathy's movements, and Nelly's chill is an unwitting factor in Cathy's secret visits to the Heights.

elysium a place of ideal happiness

gadding off wandering off to enjoy oneself

laid up confined to bed

CHAPTER 10   Three weeks later Nelly is restored to health, much to Cathy's frustration. Nelly discovers Cathy's deception. Discussion of ideal heaven between Linton and Cathy. Hareton's attempts to read again the subject of mockery. Nelly informs Edgar of Cathy's visits, which are promptly curtailed

Once again the chapter opens with a definite reference to time. Nelly is recovered from her chill and requires Cathy to read to her, which interferes with Cathy's secret visits to the Heights. Nelly discovers her secret, and Cathy confides in her the details of all her visits, most of which have been dutiful rather than pleasurable. She recounts an argument that she and Linton have had about the nature of heaven, in which she accuses his vision of being only 'half alive' and he accuses hers of being 'drunk' (p. 245).

Cathy also relates a conversation with Hareton in which he attempts to impress her with his newly acquired knowledge of reading, and she is once more scornful of the limits of his knowledge. For this Nelly reproves her.

Nelly betrays Cathy's confidence and informs Edgar of her behaviour, and Edgar forbids Cathy to visit the Heights again. However, he writes to his nephew and invites him to the Grange.

The chapter expands upon one of the central themes of the novel: the nature of knowledge. Hareton is abused for his limited skills; Nelly Dean uses her knowledge to influence events in the novel – her betrayal of Cathy's confidences has profound consequences for the health of both Edgar and Linton, though she is unaware of this as a consequence. Critics interested in the gender issues of this novel have commented upon this emphasis on Edgar and Linton's illnesses as serving to feminise them.

The argument about heaven is indicative of a reversal in the natures of the Grange and the Heights, since Linton's view is constricted and peaceful, and Cathy's sparkles and dances 'in a glorious jubilee' (p. 245) suggesting that neither Linton nor Cathy are where they properly belong.

frame invent

throstles thrushes

coned learned

sarve ye aht take revenge; serve you right

skift move

bahn going, here bound

CHAPTER 11   Edgar, realising his death is imminent, commences a correspondence with Linton in an attempt to reassure himself of Cathy's future

The chapter opens with a move of the narrative back to the present.

Nelly perceives Lockwood's fascination with Cathy, but when Lockwood forestalls her conjecture, she resumes her story once more, though even this part of her story is more contemporary, the events having happened only in the last year.

Edgar knows that his health is failing and grows increasingly concerned about Cathy's future. He is torn between wishing to die in order to be reunited with Catherine, and fearing abandoning Cathy to the weak son of Heathcliff. Accordingly Edgar begins a correspondence with Linton, Linton's part in which is closely supervised by Heathcliff. Linton too is dying, but Heathcliff conceals this knowledge and is anxious to get a wedding arranged before his chance disappears. No one at Thrushcross Grange suspects Linton's health to be as precarious as it actually is.

Once again letters play a critical and unreliable part in the sequence of events. Edgar is deceived by the letters Linton sends him into thinking that his nephew is healthier than he really is.

Edgar's confession to Nelly that he has been happy with his 'little Cathy' (p. 254) is reminiscent of Catherine's remonstrances to Heathcliff when she is dying: 'will you be happy when I am in the earth?' (p. 158). Read in the light of this it is not so much an acknowledgement of his love of his daughter as a confession of his insufficient love of Catherine.

CHAPTER 12   **Cathy and Linton meet on the moors and it is clear that Linton's health is failing, a fact which she conceals from her father when she returns home**

Another chapter which opens with a specific reference to time. Cathy and Nelly set out in late summer to meet Linton on the moors. They are astonished and alarmed at his ill-health. Linton is clearly unable to enjoy the meeting but begs Cathy to stay, and also to report to her father that she has found him in tolerable health. Linton is exhausted by the interchange and falls asleep. When he awakens he is confused and beset by voices which torment him, primarily his father's. Once he is awake, Cathy and Nelly feel able to leave him and to return to the Grange. Following Nelly's inclination they erroneously decide to keep from Edgar the extent of his nephew's ill-health.

In this chapter we are again confronted with a narrator who is unable or unwilling to read the signs. Nelly perceives that Linton is seriously enfeebled but permits neither herself nor Edgar that knowledge. This reluctance to acknowledge Linton's illness has disastrous consequences for Cathy.

CHAPTER 13   **Cathy and Nelly repeat their meeting with Linton on the moors. Linton acts as a decoy to get Cathy and Nelly back to the Heights. Heathcliff appears and reveals that he only cares that Linton should outlive Edgar. Cathy and Nelly kept prisoner at Wuthering Heights**

The following week Cathy and Nelly once again meet Linton on the moors as arranged. Edgar is by now reconciled to the union between the two cousins. This meeting, like the last, is fraught with conflict. Cathy knows she is being manipulated by Linton, but she does not understand why. Linton's terror of Heathcliff is manifest, and when Heathcliff appears on the scene he is remorselessly angry with Linton. Heathcliff confides to Nelly that his only desire is that Linton should outlive Edgar. By degrees Cathy and Nelly are persuaded back to the Heights, whereupon Heathcliff takes them prisoner. Once back at the Heights, Linton visibly improves and it is clear that his part in the plan has succeeded. Cathy bites and scratches Heathcliff in her attempt to wrest the keys from him, and his response is to beat her thoroughly, much to Nelly's indignation. Heathcliff's plan is that the two cousins should marry in the morning. Cathy pleads with Heathcliff to be permitted to return to the Grange and promises to marry Linton in return, but Heathcliff refuses her request and tells her that her father must die alone.

Nelly and Catherine miss their chance of escape when three servants from the Grange come seeking them, and they are kept imprisoned for the next four days.

Nelly reveals her legal and clerical knowledge when she reminds Heathcliff that his crime is 'felony without clergy' (p. 271).

ling heather
bespeak beg for
eft small lizard-like animal

CHAPTER 14   **On the fifth day Nelly is able to return to the Grange where Edgar is barely alive. She informs Edgar of Heathcliff's plan and Edgar decides to change his will. However, the lawyer arrives too late, but Cathy arrives back just in time to witness her father's dying moments**

Five days into their imprisonment Zillah reveals that the official story is that Cathy and Nelly had been sunk in the marsh for five days until Heathcliff had rescued them. She also informs them that although Edgar is not yet dead he is not expected to last longer than another day. Nelly is able to return to the Grange, but cannot find Cathy, who has been married to Linton in the meantime. Nelly returns to the Grange and informs Edgar that both she and Cathy are alive and well, and she implements plans to return with a rescue party to Wuthering Heights so that they might rescue Cathy. She tells Edgar of Heathcliff's revenge, and Edgar resolves to change his will so that his property can be held in trust for Cathy and her children, rather than devolving to Heathcliff. However, the lawyer arrives too late and Edgar dies without being able to change his will. He does not die, however, before Cathy returns. So the will remains unchanged and Cathy's fate seems sealed. Edgar dies with his daughter at his side. It emerges that the lawyer has been bribed by Heathcliff to ignore Edgar Linton's summons.

Since Edgar Linton fails to change his will and tie up his property in trusts, Linton is correct in his odious assumption that all Cathy's property now belongs to him (p. 277).

CHAPTER 15   **Heathcliff demands that Cathy return to the Heights since he intends to put a tenant in the Grange. He reveals his plans to be buried in the same space as Catherine, and tells Nelly how she has haunted him over the years. Returns to the Heights with Cathy leaving Nelly alone at the Grange**

After the funeral Cathy and Nelly remain at the Grange, but before long Heathcliff arrives and as master of the property informs Cathy that she must return as his dependent to the Heights. He outlines his intention to put a tenant in the Grange. As Cathy collects her belongings, Heathcliff divulges to Nelly his intention to be buried alongside Catherine, in the same coffin-space, so that when Edgar's body finally merges with hers she and Heathcliff will already be merged together. Heathcliff and Cathy leave for the Heights leaving Nelly at the Grange.

Critical attention has focused on the transgressive nature of this chapter. Certainly, Heathcliff's description of his plan to merge with Catherine is grisly, and equally it is a plan which transgresses the boundary between life and death, and between propriety and necrophilia. As Nancy Armstrong observes in her essay 'Brontë in and out of her Time' Heathcliff's plan can be interpreted as an occult dramatisation of a demonic love which utterly defies the conventions of nineteenth-century romance.

CHAPTER 16   Linton dies, and Cathy is too proud to accept the offers
              of friendship from either Hareton or Zillah, so she
              remains isolated at the Heights

Since Cathy's forced removal by Heathcliff to Wuthering Heights, Nelly
has not seen her, but she learns odd morsels of information from Zillah,
whom she sees from time to time. When Cathy arrives she is bidden to look
after Linton until he dies – a task for which she feels herself to be very ill
equipped. When Linton dies, Cathy remains upstairs in her room for a
fortnight refusing every gesture of kindness from Zillah and Hareton, both
of whom would be willing to offer her more friendship were she not so
proud. Nelly Dean's story ends here, with her unable to foresee any kind of
future for Cathy unless she is able to remarry. The narrative thus passes
back to Lockwood, who reveals his intention to give up his tenancy of the
Grange in October.

> Since Linton is a minor when he dies, he cannot will the lands that
> he inherits by marrying Cathy to his father, but Heathcliff claims a
> right to them in any case. Cathy's position as a dispossessed widow
> radically disables her from contesting Heathcliff's command of the
> property and land.

thrang busy
train-oil whale-oil (for cleaning guns)
that road in that direction, as far as that is concerned
taking rage
stalled of tired of

CHAPTER 17   Narrative returns to Lockwood and the present day.
              Lockwood takes a note to Cathy from Nelly, and
              reveals to Heathcliff that he has come to terminate his
              tenancy

With the resumption of the narratorial position, Lockwood brings the
narrative back to the present day. He agrees to take a note from Nelly to
Cathy at the Heights. Once again he is rudely received by both Hareton
and Cathy. Lockwood's clumsy attempt to pass Nelly's note secretly to
Cathy is thwarted by her assumption that it is a love note. When she

eventually learns of the real author of the letter she is filled with reminiscent longing. Once again Cathy scorns Hareton's attempts to improve his education. Eventually Hareton throws all his books upon the fire, much to his own distress. As Hareton blunders out of the room he collides with Heathcliff, who professes his pleasure at receiving Lockwood again. Lockwood however appraises him of his plans to terminate his tenancy of the Grange. The chapter ends with his self-conceited reflection:

> What a realisation of something more romantic than a fairytale it would have been for Mrs Linton Heathcliff, had she and I struck up an attachment as her good nurse desired, and migrated together, into the stirring atmosphere of the town. (p. 301)

Lockwood's deferral of real relationships in favour of the **romantic** dream have already been commented upon from the first chapter wherein he reports his holiday infatuation with his 'goddess'. He can only contemplate the (fairytale) relationship with Cathy once it is clear to him that this is an impossibility. As Margaret Homans notes in her **feminist** reading of the novel: 'Lockwood's … entire narrative is predicated on romantic desires, endless oscillations of approach and avoidance'. (Linda H. Peterson, ed., *Wuthering Heights: Case Studies in Contemporary Criticism*, Bedford Books of St Martin's Press, 1992, p. 345).

Once again Brontë reiterates the tensions and difficulties of acquiring valuable knowledge: Cathy jettisons her chance, and Hareton likewise jettisons his own, much to their individual distress.

Chevy Chase a medieval English ballad
causeway a cobbled area

CHAPTER 18   **1802. Lockwood happens to be in the locality again and is seized by the impulse to visit the Grange. He also visits the Heights where a picture of domestic bliss greets him. Nelly Dean receives him warmly and tells him that Heathcliff is dead**

This is the second chapter to open with a date, and structurally it repeats and revises the first. Lockwood is travelling in the area again and decides to pay a visit to both the Grange and the Heights. When he arrives at Wuthering Heights he peeps in through the windows to observe a scene of domestic harmony in which a beautiful young woman, Cathy, is teaching a handsome young man, Hareton, how to read. Lockwood chooses to go in via the servants' entrance whereupon he is joyfully received by Nelly Dean. Nelly informs him of Heathcliff's death some three months since, which she describes as a 'queer end' (p. 306).

The narration now passes back to Nelly and she describes for Lockwood the developing relationship between Hareton and Cathy. The relationship has been conducted around learning, both in terms of Hareton's acquisition of literacy skills, and Cathy's developing humility.

> Critics have tended to see this relationship between Cathy and Hareton as the resolution of all the conflicts of the novel, though opinion is divided as to whether the relationship constitutes a successful resolution.

frough from
wick week
mensful decent
haulf half
sartin certain
fellies male admirers
jocks jugs
side out of t'gait get out of the way
it ull be mitch you'll be lucky

CHAPTER 19 **Cathy and Hareton begin to negotiate their relationship under the hostile eyes of Joseph and Heathcliff. Heathcliff's will for revenge has diminished now that it lies within his power. Heathcliff desires to die in order to be reunited with Catherine, but feels himself to be trapped within a healthy body**

Nelly recommences her narrative with a description of how Hareton and Cathy begin to form their friendship, and the implications that their friendship has for the political structure of the household. An anecdote about them digging up Joseph's prized blackcurrant bushes in order to plant flowers is indicative of Cathy's will to cultivate the garden, and transform the Heights from a utilitarian place into a place for pleasure.

Her newfound friendship with Hareton gives Cathy the confidence to rebel against Heathcliff's tyranny. But Heathcliff has abandoned his plans for revenge and is desirous only of dying. The whole world seems to be constructed of memorabilia of Catherine, and Heathcliff feels trapped in a body which refuses to die.

J. Hillis Miller's **deconstructive** reading of the novel particularly focuses attention on the emphasis in this chapter upon memorabilia. He argues that each thing that Heathcliff encounters reminds him not of Catherine, but of his loss of Catherine. Like all texts, the memoranda are thus a memoranda to absence, not to presence: they are a tormenting reminder to Heathcliff of his failure to possess Catherine. Miller draws the parallel between this and the act of storytelling, which he observes is always after the event, it is always constructed over a loss.

lug carry

yah muh bend tuh th'yoak you may bend to the yolk; i.e., you can put up with her ways

een eyes

mattock garden implement

CHAPTER 20   Heathcliff is obsessed with dying. Finally he dies threatening Nelly that if she does not bury his body according to his wishes he will haunt her forever

Heathcliff's behaviour grows increasingly bizarre and he disappears for days at a time. When he returns, he returns in a glittery, strangely joyful mood. His manner quite discomfits Nelly, who is superstitious about ghosts and the inexplicable. When his conversation turns to making out a will, Nelly tries to convince him to repent of his former ways and turn to God. He threatens to haunt her if she does not see that his body is buried according to his wishes. Two days later she finds him dead. Hareton, who has been the most wronged by Heathcliff, is the only person who really mourns his loss. Heathcliff is buried according to his desires, against the opened side of Catherine's coffin. Local legend has it that their ghosts still walk the moors. So Lockwood hears the end of the story and on walking past the graveyard on his way home, pauses to wonder: 'how anyone could ever imagine unquiet slumbers for the sleepers in that quiet earth' (p. 334). This reveals not only Lockwood's peculiar lack of imagination, but also his continued inability to comprehend the signs of the landscape in which he moves.

The last chapter again revisits the conflict between ethical convention and a higher morality associated with consummate passion.

Lockwood's continued incompetence as a reader of signs throws into disarray all his assumptions as narrator throughout the novel, causing us to reconsider his judgements again.

rare and pleased highly delighted
chuck a term of endearment
girning grinning or grimacing: the rictus smile of death

PART THREE

CRITICAL APPROACHES

CHARACTERISATION

It is conventional to consider characterisation in terms of identity: what characterises this person? how are they identified? One of the key elements of identity might be thought to be the name, yet *Wuthering Heights* is a novel in which there scarcely seem sufficient names to go round. There is a constant doubling of names which repetitiously trace each other through the three generations of the novel. This next section will consider the characterisation of the major characters of the novel.

CATHERINE

The reader's first introduction to Catherine Earnshaw is an introduction to the signature of a ghost; her name is scratched upon the window-ledge in the room where Lockwood will have his disturbing nightmares. We cannot avoid the figure of Catherine, it is carved into the very text. At the end of the novel, Heathcliff is tormented by everything which signals to him his loss of Catherine, she is as elusive and forbidden to him as she is incomprehensible to Lockwood. Thus the characterisation of Catherine starts and ends in an enigma: the world of the novel is testament to her character, but it is testament to a character that can leave only the ghostly signs of itself behind.

The names which Lockwood finds inscribed upon the window – Catherine Earnshaw, Catherine Linton, Catherine Heathcliff – can be read as indicative of Catherine's fractured or fragmented social identity. Catherine struggles with conflicting options for selfhood as she tries to combine two irreconcilable lives: the life of passion fully experienced, and the life of social convention that secures her to either her father or her husband. Her assertion to Nelly Dean 'I *am* Heathcliff' (p. 87) is both dramatic and memorable, but it cannot stabilise her identity since Heathcliff too is enigmatic and uncertain.

The conflict that disturbs Catherine's sense of self is played out in the novel through the themes of culture versus nature. In deciding to marry

Edgar Linton, Catherine chooses culture over nature. This is directly contrasted with a narrative insistence upon her love of nature and her oneness with nature. As a child, for example, rather than read, she and Heathcliff prefer to scramble on the moors. Her diary, however, which documents the fact, pays scrupulous attention to her jettisoning of the book, but neglects to describe her impression of the moors. From Catherine's perspective nature does not need to be named, and it does not lend itself to narrative representation or culture. If we accept this reading, then Catherine's choice of Edgar over Heathcliff cannot be expected to be successful.

It is, however, in character, for Nelly Dean's first introduction of Catherine is as 'mischievous and wayward' (p. 38), thus we can expect her to make unpredictable and surprising choices. Capable of great love and fidelity, Catherine is nevertheless equally capable of ruthless destruction, even if that entails her death and wretched misery for those she loves.

HEATHCLIFF

Heathcliff is described by Catherine as an 'unreclaimed creature' (p. 101). His mysterious capacity for self-invention which defies the conventional categories of characterisation in the novel, renders him profoundly difficult to read for most of the other characters.

Unlike every other character in the novel, Heathcliff has only the singular name, which serves him as both Christian and surname. This places him radically outside social patterns and conventions. Heathcliff belongs first nowhere and finally anywhere. The fact that he inherits his name from a dead son also signals the potential for freeplay and invention, since this name might then be thought of as that of a ghost: a character who is no longer present.

Critics have most often cited Heathcliff as a **Byronic hero**: powerful, attractive, melancholy and brutal. Through most of the first volume of the novel Heathcliff's rise to power details the ascension of the **romantic** hero, with his intrusion into and transformation of a conventional and socially limited world. However, by making such romantic conventions manifest in an energetic new form, Heathcliff actually cancels out romantic possibilities and reduces that system to mere superstition. Thus in creating Heathcliff,

Brontë may well have been acknowledging Byron's influence. But in the character of Catherine she also suggests a revision of Byron and demonstrates his vision as a fundamentally male literary myth.

As a foundling, Heathcliff is introduced into the close-knit family structure as an outsider; he is perceived as both gift and threat and these contesting identifications form part of the compelling undecidability of his character. Contradiction typifies Heathcliff. To Catherine he is brother and lover; to Isabella he is romantic hero and pitiless oppressor; he epitomises potency, yet he fathers an exceptionally frail child. He encompasses vast philosophical opposites: love and death, culture and nature, evil and heroism.

Edgar

Edgar represents the world of conventional morality to which Heathcliff is the antithesis. Edgar's world is an interior world, and we first peep in on him as a child, poetically pictured by Heathcliff for Nelly Dean. Edgar's interior is:

> a splendid place, carpeted with crimson, and crimson-covered chairs and tables, and a pure white ceiling bordered by gold, a shower of golden glass-drops hanging in silver chains from the centre and shimmering with little soft tapers. (p. 48)

In the midst of this sumptuous environment, the description of which sits so uncomfortably in Heathcliff's mouth, stands Edgar, weeping by the fire. And Heathcliff despises him for his pettiness.

The descriptions of Edgar as 'a doll', a 'spoiled child', a 'soft thing' and 'a lamb [who] threatens like a bull' (p. 113) establish Edgar as artificial in contrast to the elemental descriptions afforded to Heathcliff and Catherine. And yet although there is no way that Edgar can satisfy Catherine, he nevertheless loves her in a conventional way as his wife, and when she is ill, he tends her devotedly.

It is rather a commonplace of criticism to read Edgar as effeminate, in contrast to the savage masculinity of Heathcliff. Gilbert and Gubar have reversed this trend, reading Edgar as masculine and Heathcliff as feminine. Edgar's masculinity, they argue, is that of social power. He legitimately inherits Thrushcross Grange; his books and his library establish him as a man of letters and therefore of influence. Nelly's constant reference to

Edgar as 'the master' reveals her opinion of him as someone with social power. Heathcliff on the other hand is a cuckoo with no established parentage or inheritance. His lack of formal education places him in an inferior social position.

Linton is described as lacking spirit, and this can be read in two ways. Conventionally, he does lack the vigour that characterises Catherine and Heathcliff. However, he also lacks their ghostliness, the spectral quality which sets them apart and lends them mystery. By comparison Edgar's corporeality is easy to read. He is not troubled by internal contradiction, and he remains in his place throughout the novel, living at Thrushcross Grange as boy and man, and finally resting in his grave alongside that of his wife.

ISABELLA

As Edgar's sister, Isabella's characterisation is closely associated with his. Indeed she is only ever seen in relation to other characters. Isabella's infatuation for Heathcliff, which structurally parallels Edgar's fascination with Catherine, fails to develop into a mature and unselfish love. Isabella's infatuation with Heathcliff is as a direct result of her cultural life: she can only read Heathcliff as a **romantic** hero and she never entirely abandons her fantasy of Heathcliff as the Byronic lover even when it is clear that his spontaneous love of Catherine has transformed itself into a determined lust for revenge, for which Isabella is only a cipher or vehicle.

LINTON

Linton Heathcliff is a contradiction in terms. His name signifies the unnatural union between Heathcliff and the Lintons or between passion and convention and his sickly nature demonstrates the impossibility of such a union. In Linton both love and convention emerge as corrupted by each other. Brontë reserves for Linton her most scathing imagery: he is described as: 'a pet', a 'puling chicken' and a 'whelp'.

Like both his parents, however, Linton's view of the world is singular, and it is his inability to see it in any but his own terms which renders him absolutely available for manipulation by Heathcliff.

HARETON

Of his generation Hareton's character is perhaps the most intriguing, reversing the comparative lack of interest we feel for his father, Hindley. Hareton is brutalised by Heathcliff, structurally repeating Heathcliff's own suffering at the hands Hindley.

Hareton's relationship with Cathy has similarly been read as mirroring Heathcliff's with Catherine, in as much as he is desirous of impressing her, and he is proud in her presence. His love of Cathy however, might be said more closely to resemble Edgar's love of Catherine, in as much as it is moderate yet tender, devoted yet restrained. Hareton also exhibits an unwavering love for Heathcliff, in spite of the ill-treatment he has received at his hands. Like Catherine, Hareton is constant in his initial affections, and when Heathcliff first arrives into his life they form an alliance against Hindley.

Although Hareton's name is inscribed above the door of Wuthering Heights, his inability to read, coupled with the repetitious doubling of names and signatures, means that he fails to inherit his rightful property. The structural doubling of names means that there is no guarantee of inheritance. Inheritance requires a stable system of patriarchal legitimacy and uncontested identity. Hareton is dispossessed by Heathcliff, but can also be seen as a rewriting of Heathcliff, a surrogate or symbolic Heathcliff. He is finally able to repossess the Heights only to be immediately assimilated into the cultural **hegemony** of the Grange.

The development of Hareton's characterisation revolves around his education. He is initially nursed by Nelly, the novel's surrogate mother, and under her tuition he begins to learn his letters. However, left to the ministrations of his dissolute and unpredictable father, Hindley, Hareton grows wild and uncultivated, unable to read, and with no social skills. His attempts at self-improvement are the source of mockery and derision by Linton and Cathy, and it is not until the end of the novel that he is able to acquire the skills necessary for him to achieve social status with Cathy and come into his rightful inheritance. The description of him being taught these skills is not without some diminution of his sexual potency, as he sits meekly to be alternately kissed or chastised as he learns. The domestic romance which typifies the final union between Cathy and Hareton may well resolve some of the conflicts that thwart the other relationships in the novel, but their union lacks the grand passion, the wild power of the original love between Catherine and Heathcliff.

CATHY

Structurally the second Cathy can be seen as revising her mother's story. She achieves her identity at the price of her mother's, and Edgar always differentiates her in relation to the first Catherine, whose name he never diminished. Unlike Linton, who has the misfortune of inheriting the worst of both his parents, Cathy appears to have inherited the good from both hers. She is described by Nelly as:

> the most winning thing that ever brought sunshine into a desolate house – a real beauty in face – with the Earnshaws' handsome dark eyes, but the Lintons' fair skin and small features, and yellow curling hair. Her spirit was high, though not rough, and qualified by a heart, sensitive and lively to excess in its affections. That capacity for fierce attachments reminded me of her mother; still she did not resemble her; for she could be soft and mild as a dove, and she had a gentle voice, and a pensive expression: her anger was never furious; her love never fierce; it was deep and tender.
>
> (p. 187)

This character reference from Nelly is not inconsiderable, and it influences the way we reflect upon the sour behaviour of Cathy Heathcliff as she comports herself in the first volume of the novel. However, it must be recalled that Nelly is here speaking to Lockwood, whom she sees as a possible escape route for Cathy, should he be induced to fall in love with her.

We are privy to reports of Cathy's pride, and her insensitive mockery of Hareton's lack of formal knowledge. The resolution of the novel in which she and Hareton form their attachment is something of a mythical resolution, a **romantic** conclusion which transcends the central conflicts of the novel to restore a traditional novelistic plot of courtship and marriage.

Nelly

Nelly Dean is the second and the dominant narratorial voice in this novel. She takes up the story from Lockwood and gives it both substance and credence. Lockwood's inability to read the signs of the culture in which he finds himself cannot sustain the story, though it acts to remind us that all narratorial voices, including Nelly's, are partial.

Nelly Dean is a local, and has known each generation of the Earnshaw and Linton families. She is therefore well-placed to offer Lockwood a commentary upon the events she describes. Her position of servant is differentiated from that of the other servants, both in terms of the fact that she appears to move effortlessly between the two houses, mediating between their differences, and in terms of her voice. Nelly Dean does not share a regional dialect with the other servants, although she understands it perfectly well. She also emerges as an educated woman, having read most of the books in the library at Thrushcross Grange – the house of culture – and in having experienced the vicissitudes of life at Wuthering Heights – the house of nature.

Nelly acts as a surrogate mother to many of the motherless characters in this novel: she brings up Hareton for the first five years of his life; she cares for Cathy from birth through to her marriage to Linton; she regrets the brevity of her charge of Linton Heathcliff, which is forced by circumstance; and she acts as confidant and adviser to Catherine and Heathcliff. She also acts as a mother-figure to Lockwood as she nurses him back to health. As surrogate mother Nelly provides food and moral sustenance to her nurslings.

Recurring themes

Love

Wuthering Heights has been called the greatest of love stories, and the novel's attraction as a love story is not difficult to identify. It is a novel which explores love from a number of different perspectives: domestic, maternal, social, **romantic**, religious and **transcendent**. But it is also a novel which explores that theme through a range of conventions which